CHANGE
NOW!

FIVE STEPS TO BETTER LEADERSHIP

Center for Creative Leadership®

The Center for Creative Leadership (CCL) is a top-ranked, global provider of leadership development. By leveraging the power of leadership to drive results that matter most to clients, CCL transforms individual leaders, teams, organizations, and society. Our array of cutting-edge solutions is steeped in extensive research and experience gained from working with hundreds of thousands of leaders at all levels. Ranked among the world's Top 10 providers of executive education by *Bloomberg BusinessWeek* and the *Financial Times*, CCL has offices in Greensboro, NC; Colorado Springs, CO; San Diego, CA; Brussels, Belgium; Moscow, Russia; Addis Ababa, Ethiopia; Johannesburg, South Africa; Singapore; New Delhi-NCR, India; and Shanghai, China.

Peter Scisco

Cynthia D. McCauley

Jean Brittain Leslie

Rob Elsey

CHANGE NOW!

FIVE STEPS TO BETTER LEADERSHIP

CENTER FOR CREATIVE LEADERSHIP

Greensboro, NC   Colorado Springs, CO   San Diego, CA
Brussels, Belgium   Singapore

PUBLISHED BY CCL PRESS

Sylvester Taylor, Director of Assessments, Tools, and Publications

Peter Scisco, Manager, Global Content Development

Stephen Rush, Editor

Shaun Martin, Associate Editor

Janis Chan, Instructional Writer

Design and Layout by Diana Coe, Evolution Publishing Services

WITH SPECIAL THANKS

To Dave Altman, Dawn Barts, Elaine Biech, Bill Drath, Alex Eckhardt, George Hallenbeck, Emily Hoole, Renee Hultin, Kim Kanaga, Kelly Lombardino, Shaun Martin, Marian Ruderman, Stephen Rush, Taylor Scisco, Susan Smith, and Sylvester Taylor.

Library of Congress Cataloging-in-Publication Data

Change now! : five steps to better leadership / Peter Scisco ... [et al.].

   p. cm.

 ISBN 978-1-60491-071-1 — ISBN 978-1-60491-072-8 (ebook)

 1. Career development. 2. Leadership. 3. Success in business. 4. Feedback (Psychology) I. Scisco, Peter.

 HF5381.C435 2013

 650.1--dc22

              2009031929

WHAT'S
INSIDE

INTRODUCTION VI
Your ability to succeed in the future depends on changes you make now.

MAKE CHANGES

FOR YOURSELF. FOR OTHERS. FOR THE FUTURE.

What brought you to where you are now probably won't take you to where you want to go.

If you want to reach the next level of performance or leadership,

now is the time to **DEVELOP**,
the time to **GROW**.
Now is the time to **CHANGE**.

The **FIVE STEPS** in this book will help you achieve the changes you seek.

You will **identify** where to focus your development energy.
You will **create** goals that work for you.
You will **craft** a plan for achieving your goals.
You will learn how to **anticipate and overcome** obstacles.
And you'll figure out how to **stay on course**.

Successful people have the ability to adapt. They thrive because they change.

You can be one of them.

Don't wait.

Follow the steps in this book and

CHANGE NOW!

1

PICK AN AREA FOR CHANGE

FOCUS ON WHAT MATTERS

ON WHAT CAN BE DIFFERENT

AND WHAT YOU CAN DO

BETTER

PICK AN AREA FOR CHANGE

THINK different.

ACT different.

BE *DIFFERENT.*

DO
WHAT
YOU
DO. **AND DO IT BETTER.**

Change. NOW.

The kind of leader you are is the kind of leader you want to be.

What kind of leader do you want to be?

What do you want to do better?

What do you want to do more of?

What do you want to do differently?

Twenty years from now you will be more disappointed by the things that you didn't do than by the ones you did do. Sail away from the safe harbor.
~Mark Twain

It's hard to give ONE answer to these questions. But if you want to change how you lead, start by focusing on a SINGLE area of development.

(Just one.)

Don't just pick any area for change.

(Pick carefully.)

And remember THREE things:

1 FOCUS ON A CHANGE THAT **ENERGIZES YOU.**

2 FOCUS ON A CHANGE THAT CREATES **POSITIVE OUTCOMES.**

3 FOCUS ON A CHANGE THAT IS AT THE **RIGHT LEVEL OF DIFFICULTY** - NOT SO EASY THAT YOU DON'T FEEL CHALLENGED, AND NOT SO DIFFICULT THAT YOU CAN'T MAKE THE CHANGE.

conflict management

make better use of

BE MORE

Energize My Team
Work-Life Balance

Mor

THINK LIKE SOMEONE TWO LEVELS UP THINKS

Broader View of the

GAIN EXPERIENCE

COACHING DIRECT R

Be a Culture Change Catalyst**Mor**

DEEPER UNDERSTANDING

WORK WELL WITH PEOPLE

EMPHASIZE ORGANIZATIONA

my organizing skills

PROACTIVE

Influencing My Peers

Strategic, Big Picture Thinking

Business

better relationship with my boss

EPORTS time management

Confident Decision Making

OF OUR RETAIL BUSINESS

F OTHER CULTURES

PERFORMANCE *utilize more of my creativity*

HOW TO CHOOSE AN AREA FOR CHANGE

The best way to start is by writing down lots of ideas about the areas in which you want to make changes. A few of those will come readily to mind—things you're already working on or something you've recently become passionate about.

On the next page, brainstorm some obvious areas for change. Later in this step you will rate these areas.

After you rate them, you will end up with one area for change that you can focus on.

The need for change bulldozed a road down the center of my mind.

~Maya Angelou

WHERE CAN YOU MAKE CHANGES?

potential areas for change

	Have Energy and Passion For			Will Lead to Positive Outcomes			Difficulty		
....	H	M	L	H	M	L	H	M	L
....	H	M	L	H	M	L	H	M	L
....	H	M	L	H	M	L	H	M	L
....	H	M	L	H	M	L	H	M	L
....	H	M	L	H	M	L	H	M	L
....	H	M	L	H	M	L	H	M	L
....	H	M	L	H	M	L	H	M	L
....	H	M	L	H	M	L	H	M	L
....	H	M	L	H	M	L	H	M	L
....	H	M	L	H	M	L	H	M	L
....	H	M	L	H	M	L	H	M	L

Did you miss something?

SURPRISE
YOURSELF

with additional possibilities.

HERE ARE SOME SCENARIOS TO SPARK YOUR THINKING.

What you want to change and how you want to change depend on your point of view and on your circumstances. Here are four common areas of focus as seen through different lenses. Put yourself in these situations and respond accordingly. Update the list on page 9 as you work through each situation.

BE MORE EFFECTIVE IN YOUR WORK

In this scenario, you've applied for a different position in your organization. Imagine the people making the selection asking your co-workers: "What one or two things—if improved—would have the biggest impact on this applicant's effectiveness?"

What do you anticipate your co-workers will say?

Jot down your thoughts.

Here's a different take. Think about what you are responsible for, what tasks you take on, what roles people expect you to play.

Which parts of your job stretch you the most? What parts of your job haven't you mastered? What would you improve?

Write down your answers.

Take a relationship point of view. Make a list of the key people you interact with professionally and personally. Next to each name, write down what makes it challenging to work with that person.

Do you see a common challenge among the people on your list? What can you do to deal with that challenge?

Write your answers here.

Did those questions make you think of any other areas for development? Update the list on page 9.

REALIZING YOUR CAREER ASPIRATIONS

Think one level up. Look at yourself through the lens of your boss's current responsibilities.

What would you have to change to take on those responsibilities and to perform well?

What is the primary reason behind why you might not be working at your boss's level?

Get out of your own way. Remove obstacles to your advancement.

What is it about yourself that will probably get in the way of your advancing from where you are now to where you aspire to be?

What habits do you have that might make others think you are not ready to take this job? What can you change right now to remove their doubts? What can you work on to remove your own doubts?

Did those questions make you think of any other areas for development? Update the list on page 9.

LIVE UP TO YOUR LEADERSHIP BRAND

You have a leadership brand, whether you know it or not. Other people have ideas about how you lead. From their point of view, think about what you want to be known for. Think about what other people can count on from you.

How are you different from other leaders in your organization? What makes you unique?

What can you change so that you consistently deliver on your leadership brand?

When you were a child, you probably dreamed about what you would be and what you would do when you grew up. What about that dream inspired you?

What new dreams do you have?

Do those dreams keep resurfacing?

How can you grow to nurture your dreams?

Imagine that a leader whom you admire asks to be your mentor. What are the key questions you would like to ask your mentor?

What do these questions tell you about the changes you want to make?

Did those questions make you think of any other areas for development? Update the list on page 9.

GROW FROM GOOD TO GREAT

Think of something you're pretty good at. Now imagine how you might perfect that skill.

What one thing engages you but you haven't had the time or the opportunities to focus on it?

If you could focus on it, how will you and others benefit?

At one time or another, you've probably received unexpected compliments from colleagues or from other people outside of work.

Did those comments intrigue you?

Have you ever surprised yourself by doing something well that you didn't know you could do?

Did those questions make you think of any other areas for development? Update the list on page 9.

MANY CHANCES TO CHANGE.
ONE FOCUS.

You can't address all of the areas on your list. Successful change demands a clear focus. And that means ONE area is all you need.

HOW CAN YOU TRIM YOUR LIST TO A SINGLE AREA OF DEVELOPMENT? By rating each potential area using three measures. 1) Energy and passion, 2) Outcomes, and 3) Difficulty. We will get to that in a minute.

TRIMMING YOUR FOCUS LIST CAN BE HARD. But you don't have to do it alone. Show other people your list on page 9 and ask them what they think. Write down the names of people you will consult and the questions you have for them.

Do you have **ENERGY AND PASSION** FOR MAKING **CHANGES** TO THE WAY YOU ACT OR TO THE SKILLS YOU BRING TO WORK?

How PERSONALLY SATISFY-ING OR MEANINGFUL IS IT FOR YOU TO GROW AND IMPROVE IN EACH AREA?

For EACH POTENTIAL AREA ON PAGE 9, ASK YOURSELF HOW MUCH ENERGY AND PAS-SION YOU HAVE TO CHANGE.

Mark EACH POTENTIAL AREA FOR CHANGE HIGH, MEDIUM, OR LOW FOR **ENERGY AND PASSION.**

WILL THE CHANGE YOU MAKE **BENEFIT** YOU OR **REDUCE** THE CHANCE OF **MISTAKES**? THOSE ARE OUTCOMES.

THINK ABOUT POSITIVE THINGS THAT MAY HAPPEN (OR NEGATIVE THINGS THAT MAY BE AVOIDED) IF YOU CHANGE.

FOR EXAMPLE, IF YOU CHANGE, MAYBE YOUR BOSS WILL GIVE YOU HIGHER PER-FORMANCE RATINGS.

MARK EACH AREA ON PAGE 9 AS HIGH, MEDIUM, OR LOW FOR **OUTCOMES**.

FOR A MINUTE.

Look at your potential areas for change.

Grab a highlighter or something else you can mark with.

Check how you rated each area for energy and passion and for outcomes. Highlight, circle, or somehow mark the areas that seem like the top picks.

Next, consider how difficult it will be for you to make each change.

Will the change you want to make cause you discomfort, demand a lot of resources, or in some other way make it hard for you to carry out? Things like that create difficulty.

Is it a BIG change? Does it go against your natural tendencies?

Do you have the experience, resources, and support that you need to change in this area?

IF AN AREA OF DEVELOPMENT HAS SO MANY CHALLENGES THAT IT THREATENS YOUR INTENT TO CHANGE, TRY AN AREA WITH LESS DIFFICULTY.

Rate the degree of difficulty high, medium, or low.

AND DOWN TO ONE

It is probably pretty clear to you by now which area you want to work on. Write it down on the next page. And while you're at it, mark a couple of alternatives on page 9. If you start working on your first choice and for some reason change your mind, you can redirect yourself to another area.

Congratulations!
You have completed Step 1!

Think about the change you will make and what it will bring to you.

CELEBRATE YOUR EFFORT!

Happy is the one who understands the necessity of changing to remain always oneself.
~Dom Hélder Câmara

ONE
area of change

REVIEW
REVIEW

REFLECT
REFLECT

- Focus on one area of change.
- Think about a change that will energize you.
- Think about a change that will generate positive outcomes.
- Think about a change that challenges you but doesn't discourage you.
- One **focused area of change** makes it easier to set the right goals.

MAKE GOALS THAT WORK FOR YOU

2

ASPIRE

TO SOMETHING BIGGER

TO SOMETHING MORE

AND MAKE YOUR WAY THERE

WE USE GOALS ALL THE TIME TO FOCUS TIME AND ENERGY TO ACHIEVE WHAT WE WANT TO DO AND WHAT WE ARE ASKED TO DO. THE RIGHT GOALS DRIVE US FORWARD. THE WRONG GOALS LEAVE US STUCK. MAKE A MORE POSITIVE IMPACT IN YOUR OWN LIFE, IN YOUR ORGANIZATION, AND IN YOUR COMMUNITY — AND CREATE THE GOALS THAT WILL TAKE YOU THERE.

Goals are dreams with deadlines.
~Diana Scharf Hunt

There are three types of development goals:

1 **Goals that change how you act.**

(We call these behavioral goals.)

2 **Goals that improve a skill.**

(We call these competency goals.)

3 **Goals that meet a target.**

(We call these outcome goals.)

Your challenge is to figure out the right combination of goals for the results you want.

BEHAVIORIAL GOALS CHANGE YOU CAN SEE

Behavioral goals aim at changing how you act in a way that others notice. It might be a behavior you need to stop ("stop inter-rupting when others are talking") or one you need to start ("start regularly checking in with my direct reports to see if they need my help").

Behavioral goals are the most precise type of development goal. There is nothing ambiguous about them. Other people can see the change in you, and you can easily track your progress.

When should you set a behavioral goal?

- People tell you that you are acting in a way that undermines your effectiveness as a leader.

- You avoid taking some action or another because it goes against your grain or because you don't make time.

- You want others to see that you are committed to being a better leader.

Day by day, your choices, your thoughts, your actions fashion the person you become.

~ Heraclitus

HERE ARE EXAMPLES OF

INEFFECTIVE **AND** EFFECTIVE

BEHAVIORAL GOALS

NOTICE THAT WITH THE EFFECTIVE GOALS:
- *Others can see* you working toward the goals.
- You know the times and places where you will act differently.

Ineffective	Effective
Interact more regularly with the people I supervise.	Become a better listener.
Get out of my office every day **and** talk to at least two people I supervise.	In weekly meetings, listen to others before stating my point of view.
Spend more time with my family.	Create a more participative leadership style.
Leave the office by 5:30 pm at least twice a week to spend time with my family.	When facing a key decision impacting my team, ask for input from each team member.
Deal more effectively with competing priorities.	Become a more visible leader to upper management.
When my boss assigns me a special project, talk to her about how to best fit the work into my schedule.	Each month, send a one-page update of my unit's achievements to the management team.

WHAT BEHAVIORAL GOALS WOULD HELP YOU IMPROVE IN THE AREA YOU SELECTED TO WORK ON IN STEP 1?

COMPETENCY GOALS
BUILD OR IMPROVE A SKILL SET

Competency goals aim at improving a broad ability. Abilities combine knowledge, skill, and perspective. For example, think about what it takes to delegate well: the *knowledge* of who is capable of doing what work and who can be counted on; the *skill* to give clear direction to people with differing knowledge and abilities to process information; and the *perspective* that you don't need to do everything yourself. *It might take you longer to achieve competency goals compared with behavioral goals. And other people can't see the changes you make right away.*

Knowledge is not skill. Knowledge plus ten thousand times is skill.

~ Shinichi Suzuki

When should you set a competency goal?

- You need to develop in an area beyond a single behavior, such as strategic thinking, delegation, resilience, managing conflict, or leading upward.

- You want to prepare yourself for taking on increased responsibility or a more complex job.

- Your organization has a competency model that lays out what its leaders need to know and what they need to be capable of doing, and you want to relate your goals to that model.

HERE ARE EXAMPLES OF

INEFFECTIVE **AND** EFFECTIVE

COMPETENCY GOALS

NOTICE THAT THE EFFECTIVE COMPETENCY GOALS HAVE:
- a *competency label* that describes and focuses the competency
- *performance results* that say why you want to develop the competency.

Provide better customer service.

Improve my *responsiveness to customer needs* in an effort to *increase repeat business.*

Be more detail-oriented.

Increase my attention to detail, which will *minimize my tendency to let small tasks fall through the cracks.*

Better manage organizational politics.

Enhance my *political astuteness*, which will increase my *effectiveness in my upcoming promotion to VP.*

Create more cohesive work teams.

Improve my *team-building skills*, which will *increase my effectiveness in my upcoming promotion to VP.*

Better understand how to manage conflict.

Learn to *manage conflict* to *increase my group's ability to solve problems with other groups productively.*

Create balance between my work and my personal life.

Improve my ability to *balance work and personal life priorities*, which will lead to *more satisfaction at work and at home.*

What competency goals would help you improve in the area you selected to work on in Step 1?

OUTCOME GOALS
MAKING STUFF HAPPEN

Outcome goals aim at accomplishments that move you toward your broader aspirations. For example, if work-life balance is important to you, you might set a goal of making time in your schedule to coach for your child's soccer team, or to train for a marathon. *Outcome goals are like behavioral goals in that their achievement is visible. But they are also different. Behavioral goals can bring permanent change in your conduct, and outcome goals target short-term accomplishments.*

When are outcome goals useful?

- You can identify specific activities that will jump-start the change you want to make in your selected area of development.

- You can take discrete actions that lead to the achievement you want to reach.

- Measurable outcomes are important for you and your organization and will motivate you.

Have a bias toward action—let's see something now. You can break that big plan into small steps and take the first step right away.

~ Indira Gandhi

HERE ARE EXAMPLES OF

INEFFECTIVE AND EFFECTIVE

OUTCOME GOALS

LOOK AT THESE EXAMPLES OF OUTCOME GOALS. Notice that the effective goals describe specific accomplishments or achievements and include a timeframe, but the ineffective goals are general and describe idealized achievements.

I will develop my team's ability to think strategically.

During the next year, my team will use one of its meetings each month to focus on a strategic issue facing our unit.

I will enhance the degree to which employees in my unit are engaged in their work.

On our organization's next engagement survey, my unit's score will move into the above-average range.

I will find more ways to give back to my community.

Within one year, I will have joined two nonprofit boards in my community.

I will spend more time on athletic pursuits.

Over the next six months, I'll train for and complete the Twin Cities Triathlon.

I will increase my sales performance.

By the end of this month, I will increase sales from repeat customers by 10%.

I will get the cross-functional experience I need to advance my career.

Over the next three months, I will work with my boss to identify and obtain a cross-functional assignment.

WHAT OUTCOME GOALS WOULD HELP YOU IMPROVE IN THE AREA YOU SELECTED TO WORK ON IN STEP 1?

....

....

....

....

....

....

....

....

....

....

....

....

....

....

....

....

....

....

Remember the people you identified at the end of Step 1? Ask them what they think about your goals. Ask other people too.

WRITE YOUR GOALS

In Step 1 you identified areas in which you wanted to make changes, and then narrowed your list to a single area. In Step 2, you learned about three kinds of goals.

Which kind of goals or which combination of goals will help you change?

Behavioral ▶ **Competency** ▶ **Outcome**

GRAB some PAPER. FIND a blank spot on A WALL. FOG up A MIRROR. RUB MUD on this page and SCRATCH it with a STICK.

Check
pages 29, 33,
and 37 to read what you
wrote for POTENTIAL
behavioral, competency, and
outcome GOALS.

Add some more goals while
you're at it. You can fine-tune
them later.

Follow pages 40 and 41 to trim your list of
goals to a SELECT FEW.

If you do not change direction, you may end up where you are heading.

~ Lao Tzu

Use the process you used in Step 1 to decide what area of your leadership you want to change.

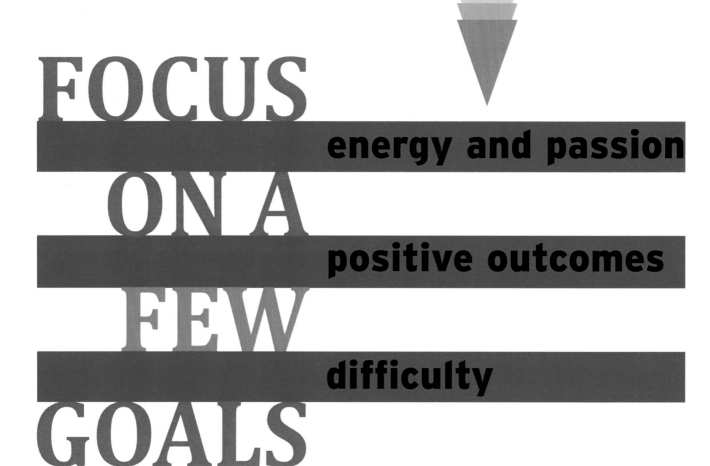

FOCUS ON A FEW GOALS

energy and passion

positive outcomes

difficulty

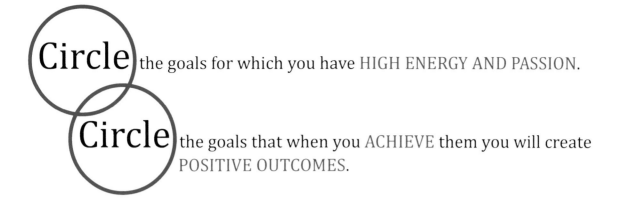

Circle the goals for which you have HIGH ENERGY AND PASSION.

Circle the goals that when you ACHIEVE them you will create POSITIVE OUTCOMES.

Consider the DIFFICULTY of your circled goals. ~~Get rid of goals that you think are too big of a stretch for you right now.~~ TURN THE DIAL UP on goals that don't stretch you enough.

Grab a marker. HIGHLIGHT the top two or three goals that you want to PURSUE. If you don't have a marker, shade the circle. DO WHAT YOU NEED TO DO to make those goals STAND OUT from the others. Don't set more than two or three goals. Your chances of success go up when you FOCUS on only a few goals.

> Put different kinds of goals in your top two or three to ACCELERATE your CHANGE. Different kinds of goals require different TACTICS to achieve and have different TIME FRAMES for accomplishing. Each kind pushes you to change in a different way. It's not a requirement to have different kinds of goals. But it is an ADVANTAGE!

CLARIFY AND FINE-TUNE
YOUR TOP GOALS

Look at each goal you're focusing on.

Is it a **behavioral** goal? If it is, LABEL it.

Is it a **competency** goal? If it is, LABEL it.

Is it an **outcome** goal? If it is, LABEL it.

behavioral	competency	outcome
behavioral	competency	outcome
behavioral	competency	outcome

I decided to be a filmmaker when I was 12. I had utter clarity that this would be my life.

~ Tom Hooper

Adjust the goals you're focused on so that each one meets the criteria for an effective goal of its type. Review pages 28, 32, and 36 for what makes a goal effective. Rewrite each goal so it is effective. Experiment with how you say it. Keep going until you have complete goals that meet the criteria.

○ **Behavioral**

○ **Competency**

○ **Outcome**

Write and rewrite the goal until it meets the requirements of an effective goal.

GOAL #1

○ **Behavioral**

○ **Competency**

○ **Outcome**

Write and rewrite the goal until it meets the requirements of an effective goal.

GOAL #2

○ **Behavioral**

○ **Competency**

○ **Outcome**

Write and rewrite the goal until it meets the requirements of an effective goal.

GOAL #3

gREAT!

You have finished Step 2! Time for a reward!

FIND SOMEONE TO SLAP YOU ON THE BACK. BUY YOURSELF A LITTLE SOMETHING SPECIAL.

YOUR GOALS MAKE UP A CRITICAL

FOUNDATION FOR MAKING THE CHANGES

YOU WANT TO MAKE.

THEY FOCUS YOUR TIME AND ENERGY.

THEY MOTIVATE AND INSPIRE.

NOW YOU HAVE TO FIGURE OUT A PLAN FOR

ACHIEVING THEM.

Take a *deeeeeeep* breath.

Slooooowly let it out.

Think about the excellent start you've made toward positive change.

REVIEW REVIEW REVIEW

REFLECT REFLECT

MAKE GOALS THAT WORK FOR YOU

Set **behavioral** goals that other people can see.

Set **competency** goals to improve a skill set.

Set **outcome** goals to make things happen.

Focus on a few goals that are important and suitable.

Write those goals so that they are effective to drive

your change forward.

-47-

3

CRAFT A PLAN

YOU KNOW WHERE
YOU ARE GOING NOW
BUT YOU NEED A PLAN TO GET

THERE

**ARE YOU ONE OF THOSE PEOPLE...
WHO IMPROVISE AND NEVER PLAN?**

good for you!

Here's some free advice:

DON'T SKIP THIS STEP.

(WE MEAN IT.)

DON'T SKIP THIS STEP.

THINK WHO, WHAT, WHEN, WHERE AND HOW

A solid plan for change includes four elements:

TACTICS (Check out pages 58-60.)

RESOURCES (It's all on page 61.)

TRACKING (Learn how on pages 63-65.)

CELEBRATING (Take a look at pages 69-70.)

There are no secrets to success. It is the result of preparation, hard work, and learning from failure.

~ Colin Powell

In our daily actions, let us concentrate on details with great care and attention, let us make this an ingrained habit for the behavior of our bodies and minds.
~ Taisen Deshimaru

TACTICS

Tactics say what **actions** you will take to **change** a behavior, **acquire** a competency, or **accomplish** an outcome.

What are you going to do?

When will you do it?

Resources come down to time,

money, and people.

What will you invest?

What is available to you?

What do you need from others?

May your soul be happy; journey joyfully.
~ Rumi

Tracking means you will regularly

check your **progress.**

How will you check how you're doing?

When will you check?

Celebrating is how you acknowledge your **progress** and **reward**

yourself for it.

What kind of reward is **meaningful** to you?

How will you reward yourself when you achieve **milestones** and

goals?

Who will you celebrate with?

UNSURE
HOW TO
COMPLETE
YOUR PLAN?
KEEP GOING.
HELP
IS ON THE
WAY.

MATCH TACTICS TO GOALS

1 **Behavioral**

2 **Competency**

3 **Outcome**

Three kinds of goals.
Different tactics for each.

1 Behavioral Goal TACTICS
CREATE CUES. BREAK BAD HABITS. MAKE YOURSELF ACCOUNTABLE.

Create cues to spur new behavior.

Put these reminders on your calendar. Your to-do list. Post them on the wall in front of you. Carry them with you. Maybe your goal is to check in daily with two people who are working on projects you supervise.

Tactic: *Post a list of project members on your wall with the question "Who will I talk to today?" in bold letters at the top.*

Break old habits that get in your way.

Think of times when you'll be tempted to not enact your desired behavior, and plan for how you'll keep those temptations at bay. Maybe your goal is to leave the office by 5:30 at least twice a week to spend time with your family, but you know that end-of-day requests from your boss or co-workers have always derailed you.

Tactic: *Craft and rehearse a response that would work in your context, for example, "My family is counting on me being home by 6 p.m. tonight, but I can get to this first thing in the morning."*

Ask others to hold you accountable.

Announce your intentions to change and ask others to let you know when you fall short. Maybe you want to stop interrupting people at meetings.

Tactic: *Tell your team members that's what you want to do and that they should jump in with their ideas first. Tell them to call you on it if you interrupt.*

2 Competency Goal TACTICS
ACCESS KNOWLEDGE. PRACTICE. LEARN FROM OTHERS.

Tap the knowledge bank.

Books, articles, training programs, webinars. Become a consumer of knowledge related to the competency you are developing. You might have a goal to learn how to manage conflict on your team.

Tactic: *Consult with your boss and HR director to identify an appropriate conflict management course. Search online for the most widely-read books on managing conflict.*

Put the competency to work.

You need practice, practice, practice to build the skills and perspectives required to achieve a competency goal. Maybe you want to increase your responsiveness to customer needs.

Tactic: *Ask to be assigned to manage two accounts where the client is very demanding. Volunteer at a nonprofit in a direct service or troubleshooting role.*

Learn from the masters.

Connect with people you consider highly competent in the area you want to develop. Watch how they work. Talk to them about their knowledge. Ask one of them to be your coach. Perhaps you want to focus on enhancing your political astuteness.

Tactic: *Schedule regular conversations with your politically savvy former boss to share situations you are encountering and get her insights and advice.*

3 Outcome Goal TACTICS
IDENTIFY STEPS. GET OTHERS COMMITTED.

Identify action steps.

Break it down. List the smaller steps you need to take to achieve the outcome. Maybe your goal is to join two nonprofit boards in your community over the next year.

Tactic: *Research the organizations in your area, contact three to five that interest you to learn more about what their board members do, develop your pitch for serving on the board of the two organizations that end up at the top of your list.*

Get commitment from stakeholders.

Figure out who is critical to your success. Gain their commitment to helping you. Maybe you want to increase your unit's score on employee engagement.

Tactic: *Talk with each of your direct reports to explain your rationale and identify ways they can contribute to increasing engagement. Enlist the support of your boss in pursuing this goal and advising you along the way.*

RESOURCES

PEOPLE. TIME. MONEY. PUT ALL THREE IN YOUR CORNER.

MARSHAL YOUR RESOURCES to implement your tactics and accomplish your goals. Think about who can help you, how much time you have, and what it will cost to get additional support materials.

Maybe you have a goal that requires **PEOPLE** who will hold you accountable, people who can provide expertise, people who will commit to your success, and people to be ready with encouragement, feedback, and guidance.

Tactic: *Take an inventory of your relationships and think about how each person might lend you support. Tap your work, community, and home networks. Talk with the people in those networks about how they can encourage and motivate you to sustain your efforts.*

Maybe you have a goal that will take you some **TIME** to accomplish. To make lasting changes, you need sufficient available time and permission to spend that time on your development.

Tactic: *Take a look at your calendar. Map out a realistic time frame that accounts for what actions you need to take toward reaching your goals. Be sure to compare your map to your schedules at work and at home to see whether the time you need is available. If it isn't, adjust your dates.*

Maybe your goal demands that you get up to speed on a specific topic, like team leadership or handling a crisis. To implement tactics for competency and outcome goals, you'll need **MONEY** for books, webinars, training, coaching, and other kinds of access to experts.

Tactic: *Create a budget to see what kinds of funds you might need—and where you will get them.*

DON'T KNOW WHAT TO MAKE OF YOUR PROGRESS? WE'VE GOT YOU COVERED.

DIFFERENT GOALS– DIFFERENT TRACKING

Make your progress notes more effective by matching them to the kind of goal you're going for.

1 Behavioral Goals

Draw up a simple checklist of questions. Answer each one at the end of every day. Try these.

■ How many times today did you act in the way you've set as a goal?

■ Did you use every opportunity to change your usual actions?

■ Did you fail to use any opportunities to change your usual actions?

■ Why did you fail in those situations?

Constantly a man should reflect and ask himself, "What good thing have I done this day?"
~ the Śāṅgadhara Paddhati

2 Competency Goals

Check in with yourself once a week. Here are some questions you can answer to record your progress.

■ What are you learning?

■ How have you developed?

■ How are you applying what you've learned?

■ Are you making progress?

■ If you aren't, what is in your way?

Whenever you choose to be mindful, you may acquire wisdom.
~ Ajahn Chah

3 Outcome Goals

Every few days write down the steps you've completed toward the outcome you set for yourself. Keep a journal or make a log on your computer.

For example, completing a triathlon means recording your running, cycling, and swimming times after each workout.

Regularly review your notes to see how you're doing.

What actions can you track that are steps toward your goal?

■ Are you making progress?

■ If progress is slow, what is in your way?

■ Where are you falling short?

Listen to the words of the passing moment: "At this moment of this long journey, where are you?"
~ Faouzi Skali

PLAN FOR THE BEST

Here is where you create your strategy for achieving the goals you wrote on page 45. As you tweak your plan, come back here and adjust your strategy.

GOAL #1:

◯ **Behavioral**　　◯ **Competency**　　◯ **Outcome**

TACTICS

TRACKING

RESOURCES

CELEBRATIONS

REVISIONS: *What adjustments have you made to this goal? When did you make them?*

Here is where you create your strategy for achieving the goals you wrote on page 45. As you tweak your plan, come back here and adjust your strategy.

GOAL #2:

◯ **Behavioral**   ◯ **Competency**   ◯ **Outcome**

TACTICS

TRACKING

RESOURCES

CELEBRATIONS

REVISIONS: *What adjustments have you made to this goal? When did you make them?*

PLAN FOR THE BEST

Here is where you create your strategy for achieving the goals you wrote on page 45. As you tweak your plan, come back here and adjust your strategy.

GOAL #3:

◯ **Behavioral**   ◯ **Competency**   ◯ **Outcome**

TACTICS

TRACKING

RESOURCES

CELEBRATIONS

REVISIONS: *What adjustments have you made to this goal? When did you make them?*

HOW ABOUT CELEBRATING?
MARK YOUR PROGRESS.

AND GET READY FOR
EVEN MORE CHANGE.

CELEBRATIONS

Making progress toward your goals is rewarding in and of itself.

But meaningful celebrations keep you motivated.

Make your celebrations significant.

Are there things you want to do but often can't because of your schedule?

Here's your chance.

What about friends or family you haven't seen in a while?

The door is open.

Make your celebration memorable.

Don't skimp.

WHERE TO FROM HERE?

YOU HAVE FINISHED THREE OF THE FIVE STEPS TOWARD PERSONAL CHANGE AND DEVELOPMENT.

YOU KNOW WHAT AREAS YOU WANT TO FOCUS ON.

YOUR GOALS ARE FOCUSED AND ACHIEVABLE.

YOUR PLAN IS RICH IN DETAIL.

NOW IT'S TIME TO CONSIDER POTENTIAL OBSTACLES THAT MIGHT BLOCK OR HINDER YOUR INTENT TO CHANGE.

IN THE NEXT STEP, YOU WILL LEARN HOW TO IDENTIFY OBSTACLES AND HOW TO MAKE PLANS FOR DEALING WITH THEM.

OBSTACLES. THEY DON'T STAND A CHANCE.

Change Keeps On Going

AN EMERGENCY OR UNFORESEEN OBSTACLE. THE DISCOVERY OF A BETTER TACTIC. A CHANGE IN RESPONSIBILITIES.

YOU HAVE WORKED HARD TO FOCUS YOUR INTENT, TO WRITE YOUR GOALS, AND TO CREATE A STRATEGY FOR SUCCESS. BUT THERE WILL BE BUMPS IN THE ROAD.

DON'T WORRY. JUST GO BACK TO YOUR PLAN AND ADJUST IT. THAT'S WHY THERE'S ROOM IN YOUR PLAN FOR REVISIONS.

KEEP YOUR EYES OPEN—THINK HARD ABOUT WHY YOU'RE CHANGING YOUR PLAN AND WHAT KIND OF GOALS WILL KEEP YOU ON TRACK.

YOUR DEVELOPMENT IS ALWAYS A WORK IN PROGRESS.

REVIEW REVIEW

REFLECT

CREATE A SOLID PLAN.

Devise your **tactics** for the actions you will take

to achieve your goals and when.

Describe the **resources** you need to accomplish

your goals—the **time, people,** and **money.**

Track your **progress** all along the way and check

in regularly to see how you're doing.

Celebrate your progress with rewards that are

meaningful to you with people you care about.

4

DEAL WITH OBSTACLES

SEE

THE DIFFICULTIES AHEAD

THE TROUBLE IN STORE

AND MINIMIZE YOUR RISK

The road of change is fraught with **obstacles**.

Difficulties can **blindside** you.

Knock you off **track**.

Frustrate your efforts to change.

Get a handle on the most common obstacles you're likely to **face.**

And plan how to deal with them.

Obstacles are those frightful things you see when you take your eyes off your goal.

~Henry Ford

GOOD NEWS!

FROM THE PREVIOUS THREE STEPS, YOU ALREADY KNOW HOW TO AVOID SOME OF THE MOST COMMON OBSTACLES.

1 YOU CHOSE WHERE TO FOCUS YOUR ATTENTION.

2 YOU WROTE CLEAR, ENERGIZED, AND ACHIEVABLE GOALS.

3 YOU DEVELOPED TACTICS TO HELP YOU CHANGE.

But there are other common obstacles, too. Keep a sharp lookout for:

TIME that squeezes promises into paste. Make time to change.

PEOPLE who may react negatively to the changes you make.

FEAR that can accompany change, STRIKE without warning, and STOP you in your tracks.

TIME

Another Day, Another 604,800 Seconds

You already pack every hour of your day. Figuring out how to fit new commitments into a busy life is challenging. If you feel a little panicked right now, then time might become an obstacle to your development.

Do you underestimate the time it takes you to accomplish a job?
- ○ Often
- ○ Sometimes
- ○ Rarely

How often do you make time to work on your goals?
- ○ Often
- ○ Sometimes
- ○ Rarely

Does everything on your schedule feel like a high priority?
- ○ Often
- ○ Sometimes
- ○ Rarely

Do you feel that you have no control over your schedule?
- ○ Often
- ○ Sometimes
- ○ Rarely

It is not a question of stopping the movement of life; it is a question of fulfilling it.

~Simone de Beauvoir

IF TIME IS A POTENTIAL OBSTACLE TO REACHING YOUR GOALS, CONSIDER THESE STRATEGIES.

Have you UNDERESTIMATED the time required to accomplish your goals? ASK other people how much time they would set aside to work on them. If they generally agree with each other but not with you, THINK AGAIN about how much time you will devote to achieving your development goals.

REVIEW your schedule. MARK your essential commitments, and DEFER, DELEGATE, or DELETE the rest. ACHIEVING your goals is an essential commitment, and now you have TIME TO MAKE CHANGE part of your daily schedule.

When you SPEND YOUR TIME DIFFERENTLY, it affects the people around you. TALK to them about how to minimize that impact. LISTEN to their opinions about how to REDUCE YOUR INVOLVEMENT in noncritical projects. Let them know how the changes you are making will BENEFIT THEM and the organiztion.

You don't have to WORK on all your goals at once. STAGE your goals to create more focus and to set priorities. START with your most important goal. If that goal is big and audacious, BREAK IT DOWN into manageable pieces. A piece-by-piece approach might slow you down a little. BUT LOOK—it's better to take more time than fail to change.

IF YOU DON'T MAKE TIME FOR GOALS, YOU'LL NEVER ACHIEVE THEM.

How will you deal with time constraints?
Grab some paper and something to write with, or use the space here.

When you spend time on your goals, how does that affect others?

What do you need to do to come up with a realistic estimate of the time you will need? Who could help? Make a list of ideas.

Which goal is your highest priority?

Which goals do you need to break into smaller chunks?

PEOPLE

Can't Change With Them, Can't Change Without Them

It's up to you to reach your goals. But when the changes you make affect other people, their responses can knock you off track.

Who might be an obstacle? Figure it out here.

Who might not cooperate with your efforts to change? Why won't they?

Who prefers that you not change because they could be negatively affected? What is the impact on them?

Will the changes you make cause conflicts between you and other people? What kind of conflicts?

IF PEOPLE INADVERTENTLY STIFLE YOUR EFFORTS, THERE ARE SOME THINGS THAT YOU CAN DO.

TELL other people why you are pursuing your goals. That helps them UNDERSTAND your perspective, motivations, and intentions. It can also HELP you get their cooperation and support. ENCOURAGE dialogue, support, and ongoing feedback while you pursue your goals.

When you SUCCEED, so do others. But it may not be obvious to other people that when you change they BENEFIT. Talk to people about the SKILLS you're developing. Help them CONNECT to your changes. WORK together. Help them to see that your growth can BOOST their performance, GAIN them recognition, and help their careers. TALK about the trade-offs, too. Don't sugarcoat it. Things will be different. No getting around that. TELL people what you need, and be prepared to support them when they PURSUE their own goals.

Supporters help you demonstrate why your goals are important and why other people should cooperate with you. Maybe your boss can be an ally. Share your goals with your staff in front of your boss. Invite your boss to describe how he or she will support your efforts. That's a positive role model for others.

{ If you need help persuading your boss or other people to support your efforts, ask a mentor or coach to join you in those conversations. But be careful. If you overuse your representatives, people will question why you rely so much on others to argue your case. }

If you make slow progress or slip back into old habits, do you worry that you will feel frustrated or incompetent?

Are you afraid that because you've tried to make changes before without success, you will probably fail again?

Do you worry that sharing your development plan with others will make you look weak?

Are you concerned that achieving your goals will have a downside you can't anticipate?

Are you obsessed with risk? Perhaps you think, "This goal is risky. If I fail, the consequences will be bad. Maybe I'm not ready."

FEAR

Breathe. Repeat after us. Fear is Natural.

Fear can disrupt any part of your development. It can be the most difficult obstacle you'll face on the road to change. It's hard to anticipate. It's hard to beat.

Fear doesn't have to destroy your efforts. Make fear work for you. But first, get to know it.

Doubt can creep into your mind when you think about your plan to change. You may worry that you lack the confidence and courage to make the changes you want to make.

Take heart.

Fear doesn't have to hold you back. You can do something about it.

Only because I err do I get it right:
I create myself.
~Orides Fontela

Practice the changes you're making in low-risk roles. **BOOK CLUB MEMBER. COMMUNITY WATCH PARTICIPANT. KIDS' SPORTS COACH. VOLUNTEER CHOIR DIRECTOR.**

Remind Yourself. Reminders are simple. Powerful. Put them where you see them. Place them where other people can see them. **THE MORE OFTEN YOU THINK ABOUT YOUR GOALS, THE MORE LIKELY YOU ARE TO KEEP WORKING ON THEM.**

LEARN TO LEARN. You made goals to learn, not to shore up a weakness. If you talk about your plan as a way to learn, people will see your efforts in the same way. People like to share their knowledge and skills. **ONE DAY, YOU WILL BE SOMEONE'S SOURCE OF SUPPORT.** Remember what you've learned here.

Watch the Downsides. Pursuing a goal has benefits and can have potential downsides. **THEY CAN MAKE YOU HESITATE.** Say you want to learn to delegate more responsibilities. When you do, how will you deal with losing control over the work? **DON'T LET THOSE POSSIBILITIES SCARE YOU.** Turn them into potential areas of change.

Look for someone to share lessons from his or her own experience. Find a person who is already good at the skill you have set as a goal. **PICK A PERSON YOU TRUST.** Your guide can give you alternative perspectives about achieving your goals. Use your guide's view on things to push back fear about trying new things.

Be positive! **EXCITED!** Enthusiastic! **IT'S NOT LIKE YOU HAVEN'T SUCCEEDED BEFORE!**

What about all those times before when you accomplished what you **SET OUT TO DO?**

Was it **LUCK?**

Hardly.

Did somebody else finish the job and **GIVE YOU THE CREDIT?**

No.

How will you deal with fear? Write down your ideas!

Where are low-risk environments in which you can practice the change you're making?

....

....

....

What reminders will you give yourself?

....

....

What are the downsides? How will you minimize them?

....

....

....

Who do you trust for guidance about achieving your goals?

....

....

....

When have you been successful? What did you do? What happened when you did it?

....

....

....

....

....

YOU HAVE A TRACK RECORD OF RESULTS.

....

Use your own history for courage to act and to change.

....

You've made great progress developing your plan.

CELEBRATE!

And then keep moving. You're almost there!

It does not matter how slowly you go as long as you do not stop.
~Confucius

ADJUST YOUR PLAN. ACT!

Ready to make some changes? Not so fast. Now that you know some of the obstacles that could knock you off track, check that your plan can handle setbacks.

GOAL ADJUSTER: What obstacles stand in your way? What will you do about them?

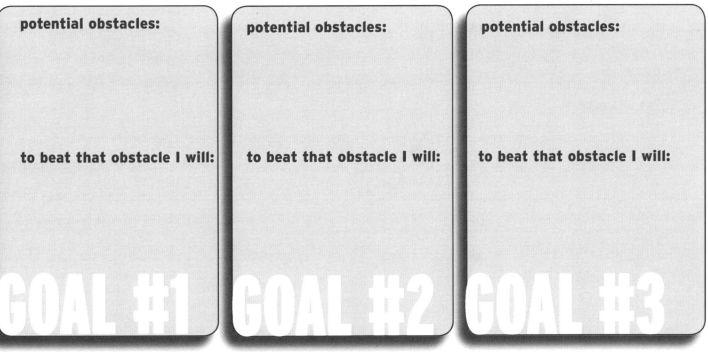

potential obstacles:

to beat that obstacle I will:

GOAL #1

potential obstacles:

to beat that obstacle I will:

GOAL #2

potential obstacles:

to beat that obstacle I will:

GOAL #3

Go back to your goal worksheet on page 45. **FIX IT.**

You are now on a path to change.

Caaaaalm yourself.

Your final step is also your first step. Put your plan into action. Track your progress. Make course corrections as needed.

REVIEW REVIEW REVIEW

REFLECT

REFLECT

DEAL WITH OBSTACLES

Anticipate obstacles to achieving your goals.

Make **time** to make change.

People will react to you differently—

some will be **positive,** some not.

Fear can **stop** you in your tracks.

5

FROM PLAN TO ACTION

CHANGE HAPPENS

WHEN YOU DECIDE

WHAT TO DO

AND ACT

YOU KNOW WHAT CHANGES YOU WANT TO MAKE. YOU KNOW WHAT GOALS YOU WANT TO ACHIEVE. WHY YOU WANT TO ACHIEVE THEM. HOW YOU WILL ACHIEVE THEM. AND HOW TO DEAL WITH OBSTACLES ALONG THE WAY.

OTHER PRIORITIES WILL TEMPT YOU AND DEMAND YOUR ATTENTION. KEEP YOUR MIND ON ACCOMPLISHING YOUR GOALS.

STAY FOCUSED!

The way to get started is to quit talking and start doing.
~Walt Disney

HERE ARE SOME IDEAS AND TIPS THAT WILL HELP . . .

Keep your eyes on the FINISH LINE

Regularly revisit your development plan. Reflect on your goals, track your progress, and celebrate your successes.

Keep your goals in the forefront of your mind.

Make your development part of your daily routine. If you don't have time during a particular day to pursue your goals, spend a few minutes jotting down some ideas or thoughts to keep yourself focused on success.

SUCCESS TIPS!

Put at least one action related to your goals on your daily to-do list. *Post visual reminders where you will see them.* Send yourself reminder e-mails or set reminders on your phone. *Create a journal for recording your daily reflections.* Write down what you're doing to realize your goals. *Take a picture.* Make a video.

Pay attention to your IMPACT

The changes you're making will affect your colleagues, friends, and family. Their responses can tell you a lot about your progress—or lack of it.

Are the changes that you're making having the positive impact on others that you intended?

You're trying to become a better listener.
Are team discussions more productive?

You're going to more of your daughter's soccer games.
Is she happy about that?

Sometimes you get direct answers. A co-worker might say, *"I appreciate the way you are taking the time to listen."* But in most cases you have to watch to see if your changing is making a difference.

PAY ATTENTION TO HOW OTHER PEOPLE REACT TO WHAT YOU SAY AND DO, ESPECIALLY AS YOU TRY OUT NEW BEHAVIORS AND SKILLS. ASK OTHERS FOR FEEDBACK:

ASK YOURSELF,

"I'M TRYING TO LISTEN MORE IN MEETINGS. HOW AM I DOING?"

"AM I HAVING THE EFFECT ON OTHERS THAT I'VE SEEN MY ROLE MODELS PRODUCE?"

RECORD YOUR OBSERVATIONS. REVISIT THEM OFTEN.

Meet Failures HEAD-ON

A great development plan and a commitment to change will take you a long way.

But no journey is free of setbacks.

Frankly, if you don't fail from time to time, then you aren't likely to make significant changes.

PERSEVERE!

To get lost is to learn the way.
~African Proverb

SUCCESS TIPS!

Learn from failure. Write down what went wrong and what you learned from that.

"Why did I fail?"

"What can I do differently the next time?"

"What might cause this to happen again?"

"What did I learn from this setback?"

If you keep failing at the same thing, stop and think. Maybe your goal is too challenging. Maybe your tactics don't work. Use what you learn from failure to adjust your plan.

ADAPT and ADJUST

Even the best plan will need adjustment. What kinds of situations might prompt you to modify your plan?

- You might change tactics or revise the timetable for an action.
- You might revise a goal or put it on hold for a time because making progress is more difficult than you'd counted on.
- You might need to drop a goal because it's no longer a priority.
- When you achieve a goal, you might add a new one.

Experiment. You don't know ahead of time what will work and what won't.

Your willingness to ADAPT AND ADJUST is critical to YOUR SUCCESS.

SUCCESS TIPS!
ASK PEOPLE WHO ARE INTERESTED IN YOUR SUCCESS FOR SUGGESTIONS ABOUT HOW YOU CAN ADJUST YOUR PLAN.

IS ONE OF YOUR TACTICS NOT WORKING? DON'T ABANDON YOUR GOAL. CHANGE YOUR TACTICS INSTEAD.

HAVING TROUBLE STICKING TO YOUR TIMELINE? MAYBE THE DATE IS UNREASONABLE. MAYBE YOU'RE PROCRASTINATING. MAYBE COMPETING COMMITMENTS ARE GETTING IN YOUR WAY. IF DEADLINES ARE TRIPPING YOU UP, MAKE YOUR TIMELINE MORE REALISTIC—BUT KEEP IT CHALLENGING.

ARE YOU DISCOURAGED BECAUSE YOU AREN'T MAKING THE KIND OF PROGRESS YOU WANT? IF A GOAL SEEMS OVERWHELMING, BREAK IT DOWN INTO SMALLER STEPS.

DO YOUR EFFORTS MAKE YOU WEARY EVEN WHEN YOU MAKE PROGRESS ON YOUR GOALS? SLOW DOWN A LITTLE. TAKE A BREAK. CHANGE ISN'T A RACE.

DO YOUR GOALS STILL ENERGIZE YOU? ARE YOU STILL PASSIONATE ABOUT ACHIEVING THEM? CAN YOU STILL SEE THE BENEFITS? CHANGE IS HARD WORK. REMIND YOURSELF OF WHAT MOTIVATES YOU.

HAS YOUR SITUATION CHANGED? MAYBE YOUR GOAL ISN'T RELEVANT ANYMORE. DON'T WORRY. YOU CAN ALWAYS CHOOSE ANOTHER AREA TO FOCUS ON OR CREATE A DIFFERENT GOAL.

WRITE ANY CHANGES YOU MAKE ON YOUR DEVELOPMENT WORKSHEET.

START SOMETHING GREAT!

GOOD WORK!

YOU'VE COMPLETED FIVE STEPS THAT WILL IMPROVE HOW YOU MANAGE AND LEAD.

STEP 1: you identified an area on which to focus your development efforts.

STEP 2: you set goals for improving in the area you selected.

STEP 3: you crafted a plan for achieving your goals, including how to track and celebrate your progress.

STEP 4: you thought about obstacles that could derail your plan and came up with strategies for handling them.

STEP 5: you put your plan into action, monitored your progress, and made necessary adjustments along the way.

Whatever you can do, or dream you can, begin it. Boldness has genius, power, and magic in it.
~ Goethe

CONGRATU

ULATIONS!

THE PROCESS YOU USED IN THIS BOOK CAN BE USED AGAIN AND AGAIN. THAT'S GOOD, BECAUSE CHANGE KEEPS YOU IN FRONT OF THE UNPRE-DICTABLE. KEEP THIS GUIDE AND THIS PROCESS CLOSE AT HAND. USE IT AS OFTEN AS YOU WANT.

BECOME THE LEADER YOU WANT TO BE.

After climbing a great hill, one only finds that there are many more hills to climb.
~Nelson Mandela

ABOUT THE AUTHORS

PETER SCISCO CURATES CONTENT FOR CCL'S PUBLISHING PROGRAM TO BRING PRACTICAL SOLUTIONS TO LEADERS AT ALL LEVELS OF ORGANIZATIONS. HE BELIEVES THAT GOOD DEVELOPMENT PLANS ARE LIKE GOOD WRITING—PRACTICAL, INTENTIONAL, DIRECT, AND, WHEN POSSIBLE, FUN.

CYNTHIA D. MCCAULEY IS A SENIOR FELLOW AT CCL. SHE HAS STUDIED AND WRITTEN A LOT ABOUT LEADER DEVELOPMENT, ESPECIALLY HOW ON-THE-JOB EXPERIENCES HELP LEADERS LEARN AND GROW. SHE IS A STRONG ADVOCATE FOR THE POWER OF LEARNING GOALS FOR ACCOMPLISHING PERSONAL AND PROFESSIONAL CHANGE.

JEAN BRITTAIN LESLIE IS A SENIOR FELLOW AND DIRECTOR OF APPLIED RESEARCH SERVICES AT CCL. SHE CREATES PRACTICAL TOOLS FOR LEADERS IN ALL KINDS OF ORGANIZATIONS. HER PASSION TO HELP THOSE LEADERS CREATE ENGAGING AND REWARDING DEVELOPMENTAL PLANS DROVE HER INTEREST IN WRITING THIS BOOK.

ROB ELSEY IS A SENIOR FACULTY AT CCL. HE ENTHUSIASTICALLY BELIEVES THAT THE JOURNEY OF SELF-DEVELOPMENT IS AN IMPORTANT PROCESS AND THAT IT DESERVES SIMPLE, POWERFUL TOOLS AND METHODS TO SUPPORT LEARNING AND GROWTH. HE LIVES BY THE MANTRA THAT "EVERYONE IS ON THEIR OWN JOURNEY."